# The Turning

# of

# The Light

By Karen Brace

# Dedication

*The world is more than we know.*

# Acknowledgements

Pauleen Cattell
Debbie Elliot
Joshua Garrett-Smith
Tony James
Michael Kennedy
Lynn & Daisy McDonald
Wyn Thomas
Andrea Wilton
Stu, Nicky & Emma

# TABLE OF CONTENTS

# The Turning of The Light

*As the year draws in, the veil thins, revealing its
mysteries,*

*Faeries dance to the Barn owl' s call,*

*The ancestors move in the half light of the memory's
horizon.*


*By firelight sain your hearth and door,*

*Open the Western gate and light a welcoming
candle once more,*

*Bid them come, among juniper and sage,*

*Pass between the bonfires to purify the way.*


*Leave offerings to honor them, let flow the fire,*

*Warm cider and beer for the witching hour,*

*The light has turned towards the end of the year,*

*Winter has come, and the spirits draw near.*

# I Will Go Into The Hare

*Violet Moon, Arcadian sky,*

*Breeze in the hedgerow, clouds pass by,*

*Look to the distance, vision dimmed by sight,*

*I will go into the hare and vanish into the night.*


*Go into the hare and flee human toil and chain,*

*Run free across the meadows in the moonlight and the rain,*

*Carrying the sight of ages, olde magick, true and strong,*


*Go into the hare and sing an ageless, ancient song.*

# Five Fathoms Deep

*Five fathoms deep, the Merrow Chieftains sleep,*

*Below ice cold waves, entombed in watery dreams,*

*Lost to the time of men, beyond the huntings and entrapments,*

*That drove them ever further into the ocean's abyss.*


*All but forgot now, to the world above,*

*Merely echoes of a time long past,*

*Carvings in ancient coastal chapels, to fright children, and old tales but half remembered.*


*In cavernous depths, they lay and rest,*

*Patient as the moon, that drives the cycles of the great ocean gods,*

*Waiting for the tides to turn once more 'gainst the legged ones!*

# The Wind That Blows The Barley

The wind that blows the barley so, gentle breeze,
seeds to sow,


Reap the land, pay your due, while the Great Wheel
waits to make the fields over as new,


Barley beer, and barley bread, sing you home and
our bellies are fed,


Weather the storm, of the winter to come,
Till the Barley King calls the return of the sun.

# *Arbo Low*

*Fallen stones, yet mighty still,*

*Lying under the Peak sky,*


*Energies of ages, pulse of the Earth,*

*Collected, stored, shared with those who chime,*


*Flow of images, journey of the mind,*

*Astral records of those who have been before,*


*Rest and remember, channel them deep,*

*In the darkest times they remain, held in the stones,*


*Wisdom of our ancestral bones!*

# The Bear and The Moon

*Sentinel of the high heavens, traveler of the sky,*
*Illuminated by the seasonal cycle of mother Luna.*

*Great protector, energy of strength and courage,*
*Bringer of dreams, olde and deep.*

*Wisdom of the ancient ones.*

*Ever entwined in an eternal celestial, shamanic*
*dance, spun of stardust.*

# Sky God

*Radial light, orb of mighty power most ancient,*

*Sentinel of the ages,*

*Born of Viracoha the creator,*

*Sitting high in your celestial sky,*

*Watching over the people of the high mountain
range and lowland flats,*

*Endlessly renewing world without end,*

*Apu Inti,*

*Wayqey Inti,*

*Churi Inti,*

*Lord,*

*Brother,*

*Son!*

# The World Through Different Eyes

*I see the world through different eyes.*

*I see you as you are, not as you would be seen.*

*Your spellcraft does not dazzle or blind.*

*Auras can not be tinted.*

*For good or bad they stand on their own.*

*I see the world through different eyes.*

*Hidden in plain sight.*

# Man or Devil?

*What is Devil, what is Man?*

*Cloven hoofed or fingered hand?*

*Darkened aspect in the eye,*

*Shapeshifting images floating by,*

*Easy to define a creature so,*

*Yet humankind recoil at the thought of knowing,*
*that Devils walk upon two legs,*

*Devil is as Devil does, as below and so above,*

*Humankind needs time to pause,*

*To re-define the Devil clause.*

# I Am The Spell

*The words that bind you to your calm,*

*Give light where there is dark,*

*Through treacherous seas and caverns deep,*

*Where monsters and daemons lurk,*

*From the gates of Hell I'd drag you back,*

*To the light of life and heart,*

*From the bowels of death,*

*Beyond time and space,*

*I am the spell,*

*The infinite spark.*

# At The Mouth of Madness

*Fragmented visions, run looped in continual suspended astral replay,*

*Time flows blood like, quickened by sudden heat,*

*Neon bright, stripping away the word clots, that clog the mind,*

*Nightmares in colour, a giant cerebral umbrella of quantum thought,*

*Firing neurons into the mind's darkest corners,*

*Done and undone, said and forgot,*

*Threads left hanging in the brain fog static,*

*Look beyond the surface, deep into the prism of each eye,*

*Delusional perception reflected back,*

*Outward calm belies the mouth of madness, screaming at the pupil's centre!*

# The Jinn

*Spirit of shadows.*

*Older than humankind's written rememberings.*

*Bringer of dark magick.*

*Chaos to your calm.*

*Force of nature, supernatural.*

*The genie in your lamp.*

*Help or hindrance.*

*Friend of foe.*

*The Jinn will find you.*

*Send Gid-dim to haunt your dreams.*

*Rouse your soul to invoke the Olde Goddess and her Red Magick of protection.*

# At The Veil's Edge

Stand with me, look across the threshold, see within,

Open your mind to the things I see,

Shadow people, faces of ancient ones gone so long,
their names have passed into memory.


Tidal energies, ebb and flow, calling to the ones
whose time is near, preparing those whose time has
come again.

A silver haloed horizon of eternal dawn and dusk,

Portal between dimensional existencies.


Sight draws the energies to the ones who channel
and practice.

A comforter to the living and touchstone for those
who have passed before.


An ever-open gateway cloaked by the modern
world's blindness to the half seen.

# Forget - Me - Not

*Tiny bud,*

*Mouse's ear,*

*Listening for the Faeries near,*

*Awaiting their call to bloom in the spring,*

*Remembrance of all that the Wheel can bring,*

*Forget Me Not now,*

*Tomorrow,*

*Forever,*

*Keep hold of the memories,*

*The Olde Ways,*

*Together,*

*Gather them in,*

*Hold gently their thread,*

*Sleep deep below ground,*

*Till their time comes again.*

# Starseed Child

*Upward gaze, scan the sky,*
*Watch and wait for the Starseed child,*

*Beyond the future, ever nearing, in time cycles*
*spiralling amongst galaxies of vast cosmic clouds,*

*Tiny atom, perfectly formed,*
*Carrying all they will ever need,*
*Smooth and pure as polished quartz,*

*Channelling thoughts of ancient wisdom,*
*Holding all close, and still,*

*Seasons pass, the Wheel spins,*
*The Starseed child longs to return,*

*Home, to the green nurturing orb,*

*To take their place in the high altar'd halls beyond
the Veil and sight of Man,*


*Waiting until the time is right,*

*To reveal themselves, step into their power,*

*And bring the world back to the Olde Ways.*

*To finish, here is the title poem of my next collection…*

# Bell, Book and Candle

*Bell, book and candle, moth to the flame,*

*Dim the lantern, polish the stones, repeat the words again.*


*Look into the distance, here but far beyond, across the Veil, into the light, where solid form is gone.*


*Still you feel their coming, whispers on the wind, gentle touch, delicate breath, you welcome, time and time again.*


*Ancestors and ancient ones, portents guide them home, rest upon my breast, until the night is flown.*

# Books by the same author

*The audio version of Waking the Witch and Other Poems is also available on Bandcamp.*

*Other ways to follow my writing journey.*

## Instagram

## Soundcloud

*The world is full of magic things,
patiently waiting for our senses to
grow sharper.*

WB Yeats

Made in the USA
Monee, IL
07 July 2026

56686371R00018